THE REAL DEAL

STUDENT ATHLETE

Success Kit

The Real Deal Student Athlete Success Kit by Tamara Statman

studentathletesucesskit@gmail.com

Cover by

Visit the author's website at www.theonlyrealt.com

First Edition

ISBN 978-1-7356120-0-3

You should not rely on this information as a substitute for, nor does it replace, professional coaching or medical advice. If you have any concerns or questions about your overall health and wellness, you should always consult with a coach, physician, or other health-care professional. Do not disregard, avoid or delay obtaining medical or health related advice from your health-care professional because of something you may have read in this book. The use of any information provided in this book is solely at your own risk.

Table of Contents

FOREWARD

I have been coaching for the past 47 years and without a doubt, you get a chance to meet many student-athletes that become markers in your career. The impact that they make can be from National Championship performances to team members that help you develop a culture of excellence that not only is about what happens on the field, but it also creates a formula for lifelong success. It is our job as coaches to prepare our athletes for life after softball [sports] and hopefully build a relationship that will last a lifetime. That is what has driven me for all these years: Watching young women come into our program and leave with skills to empower them for a successful career forever!

Tamara Statman has definitely left her legacy in our program by being a person that truly understood what hard work, vision, intelligence, and being a great teammate can bring to your college experience. She has had a huge impact on anyone that was privileged to know her and experience her optimism each and every day. You see, this was a kid that used to send me emails and sign them as the Future President of the United States! At first, I did not understand the talent that was behind the signature, but thank God, I followed my intuition and recruited her to the University of Arizona.

This book will give you a tremendous guide on how to utilize your college experience to acquire the skills to pave your road to success. Tamara was without a doubt, one of the most well-balanced athletes that I had the privilege to coach. She had a vision to take advantage of every opportunity to become well rounded in all aspects of her college career. From being a Division 1 athlete that takes a total commitment, to being involved in hosting a radio show, being active in our political system to representing Israel in softball.

This young lady did it all and excelled at the highest levels. Her advice in this book is priceless for anyone that is looking to expand their horizons during their college career and know that you can do anything if you are willing to have a passion and work extremely hard to achieve your vision in life.

I am so proud of Tamara and what she represents. Student-athletes like her come around once or twice in a coach's career and I will always cherish my relationship with this bright and talented young lady. By the way, she was also a damn good hitter!!!

-

Mike Candrea
Head Softball Coach at the University of Arizona; Former Head Coach of the U.S. Olympic Softball Team in 2004 and 2008.

CHAPTER ONE
Introduction

The life of a college student-athlete is a wild ride, regardless of what level you play at. I lived the life at the Division 1 level that you may aspire to live and while it is rewarding, the college athlete life is tough. High school and travel club teams prepare you only for a minuscule of what the college experience is like. The triple life that you live between school, athletics, and your social life does not get less difficult. The blood, sweat, and tears from practice and games will still be there and you may get pushed to your breaking point. However, at the end of the day, if I could be a student-athlete at the Division 1 PAC 12 level, you could do it too and be able to manage everything that comes with it.

Like most kids, I had to work hard to obtain a high skill set. I did not have much God-given athleticism to work with and body control was always something I had to work on; even in college. The results on the field got me noticed by college coaches, but my quirky personality set me apart from the rest. When I was being recruited, I would have hour long conversations about politics with college coaches. Speaking to coaches for an hour at a time is not for everyone, or generally advisable.

Introduction

I was already heavy into my recruiting when I was only fourteen years old, which is different from today's young athletes. My recruiting tactics included a website, game footage, and blasting it out to coaches nearly every weekend. Every email that I sent out had a signature that said, "President of the United States in 2044".

While I likely annoyed the heck out of these coaches, I certainly made myself memorable. Eventually, I landed a spot at the University of Arizona to become an Academic-All American. After college, I made my way up to international softball joining the Israeli National Softball Team in 2019.

During college, I never stopped being myself. While, at the beginning, I did not always have the most polished personality traits to be around my peers for hours on end; I was still accepted for who I was and made the best of friends.

Everything was a big learning experience and one that I would never replace for anything. The benefits of being a student-athlete make the journey well worth it in the end… when you begin to enter the real world. Being an athlete has helped increase my exposure to many different things and has proven a useful tool in and past college.

The life skills that you will take from playing sports is difficult to replicate outside of the bubble of college sports. It is a mix of not only gaining an education, but also playing at one of the highest levels for many sports. This is all while maintaining a social life and/or possibly employment. I certainly tried to do it all, but it is nearly impossible to do all four of those in sync without any bumps. However, there is still a way to get a full college experience if you are smart about it.

I was always told by counselors, coaches, and employers that the "real world " loves to hire athletes because what we lack in the job environment, we have gained by playing college sports. This also includes individual sports because there is still a team aspect and accountability built in. Many athletes have the drive, competition, and determination that has been developed deep into their personalities. This is what sets them apart from the rest.

Everyone's personal experience as an athlete may be unique, but the premise is the same for many college athletes across the country. My anecdotes are based on my experiences and you may have a completely different story to tell. There are student-athletes that may have fantastic coaches, athletic departments, and support staff during their college experience, but there are other programs that may not be the best experience for the athlete. It could include scandal and heartbreak. In some situations, you just have to roll with what is happening, but if there are situations that are immoral or illegal, including sexual misconduct or abuse allegations, know that there are people you can reach out to at your institution or at home who can help. You are never alone.

Life is not perfect and neither is being a student athlete. Just remember, your sport does not have to be your whole life. Do not let it define who you are as a person. Your sport is something you do, not who you are. For me, sometimes softball was in the middle of my list of things I was concerned with, usually in the off-season. I was involved in so many different things all the time I did not even know how many organizations I was a part of. Granted, there were many times where I had to step back from most activities during softball season or when everything became too much.

It was important for me to try the things I was always interested in, but not able to do. Pursing those activities was how I got my full college experience.

Just like every part of life, you learn from your experiences. I wanted to share tips and tricks so that other student-athletes could begin with a head start and understand what is to come. While I give you a quick snapshot of everything, there are certainly many more experiences that go into being a student-athlete.

During my time, I was able to hear stories from student-athletes across the country to understand how all of our experiences can differ. My experience at the University of Arizona (UofA) could certainly be different from another's experience, but overall, I do believe nearly all staff at these colleges do have our best interest at heart when it comes to producing quality people and accomplished scholars. Having a support system of friends, family, and athletic staff is essential to be successful at the college level. There is no "one size fits all" for each individual, but it is important to have a few close people you are able to express yourself with.

As you grow as a person throughout college, you will change and so will other people. Sometimes the people that you knew in high school will not talk to you. Other times, if you perform well, especially on television, you may find people reaching out to you through social media just trying to be associated with you. There are some acquaintances and friends who come and go and that is okay because people are ever changing. Just know that your teammates are there for you and often are going through similar experiences.

Never forget that the first part of student-athlete is a student. You are a student first. Do not forget that; while it is the one of the last things that I mention in this book it is one of the most important parts of playing college because technically you will be getting an education with the help of your athletic abilities. I came into college with enough credits to be a sophomore academically. My junior year, I pulled a class so I would not graduate early and I took up a third minor (that I eventually dropped) to graduate with my class. I wanted to play a fourth year of softball to have the chance to go to the World Series and take classes that interested me beyond my major.

Yes, college can be a jump for those who are in sports like men's basketball, football, and baseball, but remember, eventually your athletic career will end. You will likely have to find something else to do. School will always be there. Especially for those who went to the "league" and want a second go around at school.

Collegiate athletics is the biggest wild ride that you will ever embark on. Success, disappointment, and drama will inevitably ensue during your career. You will experience the highest of highs and the lowest of lows. There is nothing worse than disappointing your team and nothing better than seeing your team explode with excitement. You will try to figure out how to make your life work around your sports schedule. It is on a rare occasion where a life event will allow you to leave your team, especially during season. Other than that, expect your sport to be the biggest part of your life.

I made my commitment that I was going to uphold the standards of the UofA at fifteen years old. I knew from the moment I verbally committed that I represented my future institution. Every decision that I made could reflect back on Arizona. That is a lot of pressure to put on a fifteen-year-old.

Today, recruiting is much different and thank goodness for that. There were seventh and eighth graders making the life changing decision of where they would attend college. By the time they were ready to sign their National Letter of Intent, sometimes it was not to the original school they committed to. There would be coaching turnover or priorities may change for either party. I was a sophomore when I made my decision, but luckily, I was among the few who knew what they wanted to study.

Introduction

Your sole decision of where you go to college should not be who the coach is. It will certainly be a large factor, but it should not be the only reason. Coaching changes happen, and if it happens while you are in college, the first thing you should think should not be to transfer schools. When I was taking my college visits, I asked the coaches if they intended on staying. Of course, they all said yes, but one of them wound up leaving a year or so later. I planned on picking a school where they had my major, it felt like the right social environment for me, and I would feel comfortable even if the coach left.

Do not take the decision of picking a college lightly. What you will study, the people that you will play with, and even the weather should also be a determining factor. I cannot stand any weather below 75 degrees, so by default I ruled out schools back east and up north. If you are considering a school in a colder climate and you are from a warmer climate, take a visit during the winter and see if you really like that school enough. Your opinion could change.

Never forget that playing college sports should be fun; even though it certainly does not feel like that most of the time.

Sometimes, the love of the sport ebbs and flows. There are days you may love it and days you may really hate it. However, if playing the sport becomes a unbearable there may be a few things you need to assess. The first thing being that it may just be an off year with personalities between you and your teammates. I have been on teams where one year was not so good and the next year it was awesome. Second being should be to assess whether the school you are at is the best option; sports program, school, and everything else. The third thing to look in the mirror about would be if you really love your sport enough to continue. Some people simply just get burnt out.

In the end, you need to make the best decision for you and your playing career, academics, and personal life.

As a student-athlete, your time will be spread thin, but if you use it effectively you will come out a rockstar. Even if you wind up not finishing college as an athlete, it is essential to use your time productively. Take the extra time you have to network, join clubs, apply to internships. If you do not have some of these extra things on your resume, you will be a harder sell to an employer after college. People love to hire student-athletes, but if you have the extra oomph on your resume, that will separate you from the rest. I ultimately wrote this guide so you are able to learn from my successes and mistakes in order to better yourself during your time as an athlete and beyond.

CHAPTER TWO
Working Out

The competitive training regimen that you do in college, depending on the program, will be some of the toughest you have done in your life thus far. Working out is typically how you may begin or end your day, so just prepare yourself mentally for that. I did not lift a weight until I got to college and quite frankly, it was not necessary for me to do so. However, it does depend on your sport and program because I did have to show up to campus in running shape. If your school says lift before you get to college, you should lift before you get to college, but make sure you are taking proper safety precautions when you do. If it is not safe or available, find an alternative.

During the fall of my freshman year, the trainer had me start off with the weight room intern who would oversee me since everyone else had introductions during the summer. I did not really know what I was doing, and I simply was not strong enough to hold the 20/25 lb. weights. I would be lying if I told you I did not shed some tears during the workout. It was just hard and something I was not used to. I did not want to look like a wimp to my teammates, but lifting for me just sucked. I hated it.

However, the growing pains did not last long. After a month or two in the weight room, I was feeling more comfortable and was no longer the last person to finish workouts. While it was a huge learning process, I was able to get to similar weights as my teammates by the end of the fall. The weight room is a place to learn how to use your body in a different way and become faster and stronger than you were before. Everyone at the college level is lifting and conditioning. It is all about who has the competitive advantage.

There were even times as a junior and senior where I was given crap in the weight room for not being able to carry the same average weight for dumbbell head holds. Another time, the same thing happened with not being able to lift a landmine with a 45 plate on it with the quickness and strength as my teammates. It happens, but you have to be able to accept the challenge. You will get stronger and as time goes on you will see progress. As an overarching statement, you will need to accept the fact that you will be sore all of the time. It is the nature of the beast between working out, practice, and other activities throughout the day. It is all about who can push through that soreness to perform every day.

As a team, it is necessary to face adversity together. In the off-season, that will come in the form of testing or workouts. The term "hell week" is usually assigned to consecutive days of workouts/testing combined with practice. To add onto this, many schools are now adopting "military-like" training programs, where the team is put to the ultimate mental and physical test for a few days. I was a senior when our coaches decided it was important for us to take part in an exercise like this. While the workout in itself was not necessarily the hardest thing ever, what made it so challenging was that everyone had to do everything together. No one could be out of sync and directions had to be followed exactly. Not only were you accountable for yourself, but your teammates; just like when you play your sport.

These training sessions are perfect to get a team working together. You do not have to like every person, but in order to get things done you have to respect them and how they will help your team move forward. If someone is not doing something effectively, you have to tell them, or else the individuals running the simulation will likely make your team start over. You will learn how to try and try again until things are done right. It is a great precursor to any pre-season because it establishes a precedent for the team. The precedent, whether you go through an experience like this or not, should always be to do things with a purpose and as a team.

When I engaged in this process, I saw a miraculous change in the team dynamic. It is a tough thing to go through and having your teammates there makes it much more bearable. Our team was able to have real conversations when something bad, like drama, came up. This could be simply someone saying the wrong thing at the wrong time or a clear dispute between two people. Your teammates are there for you and you all should be able to genuinely engage in conversation and encourage each other, especially during the hard times of the weight room and conditioning.

While working out at a gym can be a challenge at times, not being conditioned is the single lamest excuse that you can have when you go to your program. You can run anywhere; especially when many conditioning tests require 50-100m of space. There were many times where I was at home running in the street or if I was on vacation, in parking lots. Testing is the single largest giver of anxiety to student-athletes. Many are afraid of the consequences if they fail. One year, during testing, baseball was playing metal music in the weight room and that shot my nerves up so high I was almost ready to pass out. However, if you put in the work beforehand, trust yourself that you should be fine during testing.

When it comes to which tests matter the most, it depends on the school and program. Sports like softball and soccer may have a large emphasis on the conditioning tests, but other sports like the track and field throwers may have a focus on the weightlifting tests. I can only speak from experience as a softball player, but the conditioning tests were the most important. They would also change every year and we would continually practice and test them throughout both semesters. Sometimes our trainers would try to pull a fast one on us and change the test when we get back to school. As long as you prepare effectively for whatever they told you that you would do originally, you will be fine for whatever else they throw at you. Which happened in my case.

One big part of passing testing, when I was at Arizona, was earning our “A”. This was based off of how we did in testing, attitude during practice, and practice/game performance. The beta year of earning the “A” began my freshman year. Having your “A” is a big deal because not only do you really feel a part of the team, but it is also when you would get all the cool clothes and gear like the “athlete backpack”.

Even though every player only had to earn their “A” once, it did not mean it could not get taken away. During my junior year, there was a significant amount of my teammates who were just unable to pass testing. Coach took away their “A” until they were able to pass testing and fulfill requirements of being a good teammate.

Not having an “A” meant that those teammates had to wear blank shirts. All of us who had our “A” wore our shirts inside out in protest because we wanted to be together as a team. Coach commended us for that, but said that was not the point of them losing it. Eventually, my teammates were able to earn their A's back and we were finally able to truly be all together. If your school has a program like this, it is essential to trust the process. It may not seem fair all the time how someone could earn their "A" before you, but in due time, you will earn it and it will be fulfilling

Just because the work is over during your offseason or pre-season does not mean you get to sit around during breaks. Working out during summer and winter break is important. This is the time that makes or breaks people. It is, however, essential to rest your body. Your body is likely to be extremely exhausted from all the lifting, conditioning, and playing by the end of each semester. It needs a break to help protect from overuse. The days of break go by quickly so do not make the mistake of prolonging your rest to where you cannot prepare yourself for testing.

If your sport is during the spring, over winter break you can have a few days off, but I would recommend following your workout program as soon as possible because your season is around the corner. For the summer, take a couple weeks off and then ease back into the workouts (as long as you are healthy). If you play a fall sport then flip the recommendation as soon as your season ends. Typically, your athletic trainer will be able to recommend how much time you should take off before or after your season.

During a long break, it is imperative that you ease into the running workouts. You will feel much better doing it that way. Do not try to go ham all at once. Your body will be extra sore and mad at you if you do that. Being able to enjoy some of your last summer breaks is certainly a priority. Laying in bed or walking around in pain because of what you put yourself through should not be a majority of your summer.

If you plan to be in a place where you may not have access to gym equipment during the off season, you will have to talk to your trainer about alternative workouts. Do not just not do the workouts, that will likely not go over too well. One summer, I was playing softball in Israel for the Maccabiah Games and I knew I would have extremely limited gym equipment and space. After speaking to my trainer, he told me to do certain bodyweight workouts and running workouts. Luckily, I played a sport where we do not necessarily need the gym all the time. However, I was still running up and down the staircase in the hotel like a crazy person. Luckily, I never passed by too many people who saw me working out.

My trainer was able to set me up for success because he knew I was in a place where I did not have the same training equipment as usual. Having open communication is required because no one is able to help you if you do not communicate.

One year, Coach made us have accountability partners during winter and summer break. We were checking in with our partner a few times a week to make sure they were doing their workouts. That year, to make things even more interesting, we did the running testing with our partner. If my partner did not pass, I did not pass and we had to run it again together until they passed. It created a greater sense of teamwork added to something that is typically individual. The attitude of testing can often get individualistic with the only thought going through your mind is to just pass the test. When accountability partners were thrown in, testing became about the "we" instead of the "I". The running sucked either way, but you felt more involved because you were running for the other person.

Working out is fortunately/unfortunately (depending who you talk to) a huge part of college athletics. It is something that will give you a competitive advantage if you put your all into it. It will be tough, but it is worth it in the end for the results. You will be in the best shape of your life. Our trainer would always tell us that the workouts that we did would not give us abs, but we would be in the best shape for our sport. My teammates and I were always sad about that, but we were doing the essential things to get the best results that would pay off in the end. Luckily, now that I am done with college sports, I can work out however I would like. Yet, all those years of being a college athlete does not leave me and I am able to take what I learned and apply it to my workouts now (or not) depending on my preference.

CHAPTER THREE
The X's and O's

Practice is the worst and the best part of the whole college of experience. Some parts of practice were really beautiful to watch because of the execution by my teammates. Other parts of practice hurt my eyes and my heart because I knew we were about to start running. Love it or hate it, it is a part of the experience. You are committed to completing thousands of hours of practice and you have to embrace being comfortable feeling uncomfortable.

Practice is fun sometimes because of how smooth the whole practice goes. Typically, these practices do not have a lot of mistakes. Everyone is where they are supposed to be and is consistent in their work. Sometimes when Coach was feeling quirky, he would spark some competition for us. Sometimes he would have outfielders try and hit a bucket at home plate or make up another type of challenge. These are the absolute best when these challenges do not have consequences because the fun competitive spirit comes out; Coach may even crack a smile or some jokes. Most of his jokes were muttered under his breath and probably were not actually jokes, but it was some of the funniest stuff that you could hear.

However, there were times when Coach would use "competition" to wreak havoc, the rewards could be good, but the consequences were certainly fatal. For example, there is a game called "21 Outs" because a full game of softball has 21 outs. Essentially, the team in the field is against the clock and has get 21 outs before the timer runs out. Every time a mistake happens, the outs start back at zero. The number of outs that we needed to get was how many foul poles we would have to run after, which could potentially be a lot of running back and forth. There is a huge pressure to be perfect because in this game, you have to be.

My freshman year, 21 Outs was a game that I heard about from all the returners. They would whisper the name with hope that we would not play it. When we saw that Coach had 21 Outs in his practice plan, everyone became much more timid and anticipatory. When we got to that part of practice one of the assistant coaches had her timer and we were off to the races. Throughout the game, the numbers would fluctuate to where we would start over with disappointment. As the game went on the tensions got higher. As the time was running out, we got all the way to 20 outs, but someone messed up. We started over, got one out, and then the timer ran out. That day we ran 20 foul poles.

In my four years, we only played that game the amount of times I could count with one hand maybe two. The only other time we had to run because of that game resulted in three foul poles. There was nothing worse than the petrifying fear of running foul poles because we were not able to complete the challenge. There is no better feeling on earth than beating that game because it would give everyone nightmares if we did not. Everyone would simply be elated for the rest of the day if we beat that game.

21 Outs is just one example of challenges that your coach could give you in a different context. The feeling is all

the same...being on-edge with adrenaline going through your body. During practice, your coach is trying to put more pressure and increase the speed of the game than what would typically occur during games. They want it to be more challenging so when you go into your game or match it feels routine. Coach would always tell us that practice was harder than the games and it should be that way. Games/Matches should be where you trust your training and just have fun.

The goal for practice, no matter if you are playing or not, should be to get better. Every single day and it does not have to be momentous strides. The goal should be 1% better, but if you can only get .5% better, that is better than nothing. However, we are human and that does not always happen; sometimes there are steps back before going forward. There were times where I was failing over and over again, but eventually the 1% better came through. Do not let the bad times discourage you. The seasons are reasonably long with a lot of gameplay. Looking too far ahead will not get you very far; take everything day by day.

Every individual has different ways they like to practice outside of team practice. Some people do extra, others do not. It is all about what you personally need. Sometimes a little extra does not hurt. However, there can be times when you can practice too much. You have to know when you need to stop. Oftentimes, freshmen do not know when to stop. It takes time to find out the limit, but it is important to know where that is. In my case, it was practicing hitting or pitching just to the point where it was not beneficial anymore. I had an upperclassman, who had a similar problem, to be able to guide me to when extra work was no longer beneficial.

My freshman and sophomore year, I felt unstoppable because I was for the most part consistently playing. The tables turned my junior year and I do not know what happened, but it was something I had to work through. I also got the flu that year, that kept me out of practice and games, to add more insult to injury. That year was tough, but I was still always ready to play. I was waiting for my number to be called to pinch hitter. However, there were also three other girls who could have been called as well and no one ever knew who would be the one called to hit until that moment. No matter who was called to hit, it was devastating to who was not picked because of how badly everyone wanted to get even one at bat.

My senior year of college was on and off. By the middle of the season, I was starting more frequently, but then a wild pitch to the face took me out pretty much for the rest of the season. I was cleared and ready to play after a couple weeks, but by then I was already out of the rotation for a starting spot and waiting for my chance to be a pinch hitter.

Just like the previous year, I was still going to be ready in the off chance that Coach was going to put me in. It paid off in the postseason regional semi-finals when I was put in to pinch hit with two on base. I just needed to control the controllables and do what I could do for the team to put us in the best position to get ahead. I hit a single up the middle to score both baserunners. It is a great feeling and if I was not ready to be put in that position; being successful would have been more unlikely.

When you are playing and playing well. It is the greatest. You get to experience the cheers of the crowd and the potential glory of game winning plays. However, your spot is not permanent. It can be taken away from you for any reason, whether you know the reason or not. I have seen instances when an individual who played nearly every game was pulled because of a bad attitude. In most cases, no one is immune to being pulled. There are some people who seem like they are the coach's favorite and are always starting, but even they could have a bad outing (or multiple) that result in getting pulled eventually.

It is not fun to not play, but you have to embrace what is happening and take it for self-improvement. You need to be able to make the most out of your situation because you never know when your number could get called to play. There is light on the other side of the tunnel. You cannot control what your coach does or says. They make the lineup, not you or your teammates. It can be difficult to embrace a role that you are not comfortable with regardless of whether you are starting or not. Sometimes you just have to suck it up and take up the challenge. Nothing comes easy, so stop acting like it does.

CHAPTER FOUR
Surviving the Grind

It truly takes a village to raise a college athlete into a young man or woman who is ready for the post-college world. Taking care of your body will be by far one of the most important ways that you will be able to survive whatever is thrown at you both mentally and physically. The grind is a very real thing and being able to navigate it effectively will ensure that you will be able to take on multiple years of this type of strain.

One of the secrets for many is naps. I was never a napper and could never get into the sweet spot of taking naps. It really just was not my thing, though, half of my team were big believers in naps. Some would even take them before games! There are still important rules to keep in mind when it comes to napping. First, make sure to set an alarm and make sure it is set to the correct time of day. This goes for waking up for early morning practice and naps! If you have trouble getting up, put the alarm somewhere where you would have to get up and turn it off; rather than just roll over and hit snooze. Another alternative would be napping in the team room/locker room. That way, someone will see you and wake you up if you oversleep or you can ask them to wake you up before practice starts. Let one of your teammates know where you are if you are not sleeping in the team room.

Just in case. Personally, I had my phone alarm and a cheap $5 digital alarm clock as a backup just in case. I was just really paranoid that I would oversleep. I definitely annoyed all my roommates because I would forget to turn the digital alarm off after I already left the house.

One time, a freshman was taking a nap in the dorm before practice. She was known to be a serial sleeper, but usually we do not worry about people oversleeping for midday practice. As the start of practice began to creep up on us, we started to get worried about where she was. By the time practice started, we informed the coaching staff that she was not answering her phone and no one knew of her whereabouts. One of the assistant coaches went to her dorm, woke her up, and brought her back to practice. Needless to say, she ran for most of practice. She was one of those individuals that was a heavy sleeper and oftentimes did not wake up to her alarm. From that instance on, she would then strictly take naps where other teammates would be.

When it comes to having fuel in the tank, you do not want to be running on no energy, especially with early mornings and late nights. You will need to sleep. My goal was to get at least seven to eight hours each night, going to bed at 10 pm and waking up at 5:45am for 6:30am workouts. Did I really typically hit my goal? About half of the time, but one could dream. Sometimes, I did not use my time efficiently and stayed up until 12 am studying, just messing around on my phone, or hanging out with people. It happens, but try not to do it often. I did have teammates who did go to bed early at eight, if possible, on regular practice days. It truly depends on the person and the amount of sleep one could function on. Regardless of the amount of sleep you believe you can run on, it is important to sleep more than enough so your body is able to rest and recover. You do not want to burn out.

Not only is recovery based on sleeping, but it also encompasses what you are putting into your body which can help or hurt it. You need to make sure that you are eating. Some schools have strict diets that limit what you are allowed to eat, but make sure you are getting enough calories to function. Luckily, I was at a program where we had a see-food diet. While we had a nutritionist who would oversee what we were eating on the road and for pre-game meals, we still had free reign on what we were eating at home.

Not every school is like this; some programs have strict "diets" that coaches may prefer you to be on. This could be to limit intake of sweets or other unhealthy foods. Regardless, it is important to fuel your body with food that will help it run.

Luckily, we often got meals provided to us after practice, but not every school is like that. Money can be an issue when it comes to being able to afford enough food on a tight college budget. If you have food insecurity, do not be afraid to reach out to your coaches, trainers, or school/community organizations for resources. Food is important to your overall mental and physical health. You need to eat. Skipping out on meals or overexercising will not help you in the long term for your personal life or athletic career.

When it comes to your overall well-being, many universities offer psychiatric services. Do not hesitate to use these services. Some athletic departments have sports psychologists and sometimes even clinical psychologists built into their training staff that you are able to see within a very reasonable timeline. While getting psychiatric help may seem like a very vulnerable thing to do, the ups and downs are too extreme sometimes to not visit. While not everyone sees a psychologist, make sure that you have a trusted individual that you can go to talk in confidence about life or team issues. It will help and this individual could be an academic counselor, trainer, even coaches.

Along with taking care of your health, if you are an outdoor sport, do not forget to put on sunscreen. Athletes are extremely susceptible to getting skin cancer later in life because they are out in the sun for nearly four hours a day of practice for at least eight months of the year. Sunscreen is so important to be able to protect your skin from the dangers of skin cancers like melanoma. I would always wear long sleeves underneath my practice/game uniform because I really wanted to limit the exposure of my skin to the sun. Sometimes I would have to reapply the sunscreen because of how long practices would be. When I was in high school, I had an atypical mole removed by a Mohs surgery and from that moment on I became a big skin cancer prevention advocate.

In college, I tried to promote the use of sunscreen, hats, and long sleeves to my teammates. Sometimes, their sunburns would get nasty and peel either from not protecting their skin during practice, or from laying out and tanning in their spare time. There is no such thing as a safe tan and you should certainly be protecting your skin if you are outside so much.

Once during summer softball camp, I was wearing shorts with long socks and I forgot to put on sunscreen. The backs of my legs turned into lobster red and it was painful. Good thing I was not really playing softball, just mostly overseeing the campers.

During games, there are a few handy tricks to keep yourself going strong. The first thing would be to always have snacks in your bag. You never know how long a game will last and you do not want to be running on fumes with no refuel. My teammates and I would always carry gummies or granola bars to munch on halfway through a game. If your sport does not allow you the liberty of having longer time outs or off time to really enjoy a snack, something that could be quick to snack on if needed, such as nuts or raisins. Otherwise, still pack some snacks for between games or matches. You will need it. Typically, double headers meant that we would eat peanut butter and jelly sandwiches.

If you are sitting out of the game/match, do not allow yourself to have a crappy attitude. It does not look good or incentivize your coach to want to put you in. Cheer your teammates on. Make their successes your successes. It will help keep you engaged in what is happening in the moment. It is tough to not want to throw yourself a pity party. However, doing that does not do anyone any good. Just be in the moment and ready for anything. You never know when you could be called in to play.

My senior year during post-season regionals, was an example of being ready even if you are not starting. I was always engaged in the game even if I was not playing because no one ever knew who Coach would put into the game to pinch hit. In the semi-final game of our home regional, my number was called to pinch hit with multiple runners in scoring position. I was able to hit a ball up the middle to break open the game and score the only two runs that we earned. Winning this game allowed us a seamless entry into the finals of our regional. It was crucial to be engaged otherwise I would have never been able to make an informed decision at the plate.

When you are playing, just like when you are not playing, have a good attitude. This should be a given, but it puts you in a much more favorable position with your teammates. Do not be that person who has a terrible attitude even though you are playing. The others who are not playing would certainly like to be in your shoes. I have seen Coach pull a regular starter out of a game because of a bad attitude. This was one of those players that I have never seen her not be in a game. Coach may have felt it was important to show that no matter how good you are, if you have a bad attitude it does not matter. While everything will not go your way and sometimes passion takes over your emotions, it is important to be mindful of what you are doing. Do not break or punch things. It will not make anything better and you may hurt yourself. You may have to tell your teammates how to interact with you or not interact with you if your emotions start to boil. It is better to be ahead of the curve with dealing with others than to potentially let it escalate to another issue later.

The biggest piece of advice I could give any incoming college student, athlete or not, is to learn how to use time effectively. All of the freshmen have required study hall, typically, and some continue to have required study hall after their first year. Take advantage of that as much as you can. Study hall was a place where I was able to make friends and hang out with my friends. However, when it came down to doing work, I did not waste time doing other things such as watching tv shows. If your friends and teammates become too distracting in study hall, either put in headphones or distance yourself. Do not do yourself a disservice by wasting time and then having to do your homework later when all you really want to do is sleep.

To ultimately survive the grind, you want to put yourself in the best position possible mentally and physically. This includes making the right decisions. While the right decision may not always be the easy one, it will be worth it in the end.

CHAPTER FIVE

Talking To Your Coach

Your coach, at the end of the day, wants to be your biggest cheerleader. You would not be at your program if someone did not believe in you. Speaking to your coach could be some of the scariest things you do, especially if you do not have a good relationship.

I was extremely lucky to be able to play for one of the most legendary coaches of all time, Coach Mike Candrea. He is the John Wooden of softball and I got to learn from him nearly every day of my career. Through the roller coaster of life and the season, Coach is always rooting for all of his players to do well both on and off the field. This is even after our playing careers are over.

While I had a good relationship with Coach, I was still nervous most of the time when I went into his office until my senior year. I would often force myself to hello and take some of the chocolate he had in his office to try to get over the nervousness.

I honestly think that coaches put candy in their office so you go in and talk to them. That or they just really like candy.

When I went to Coach's office with a purpose, like talking about my swing, it was a little less scary because it felt more educational and I knew what we were going to go over. Every single time I went to his office, to ease tension, I would find a new knickknack that he would have in his office. He had a lot of things on the walls and in cases in his office. Over the years, Coach would casually mention that he put something new in the office and I would try to figure out what the item is.

Some athletes have a neutral relationship with their coaches. Conversational interactions could mainly be limited to entrance and exit interviews every year, rather than striking up conversations before practice or going into the office to talk. If this is the case, you may feel weird talking to someone you may not necessarily know well, personally, even though you see them everyday. If you do not talk to your coach often, you may not know how they may react to requests, comments, or concerns. Regardless, take a deep breath before you step into the office, walk in there confidently, and know that you belong.

You do not have to be your coaching staff's best friend. It is important to have a relationship so you are able to be comfortable to tell them information from school to personal life if you need to. You do not have to divulge all the juicy details, but if it feels like the right time or place, you should feel comfortable enough to get advice about anything from your coaches.

Not everyone is able to get on this level, but it is important to at least be on the same page as your coach about what they expect out of you. As an athlete and a person. If you do not agree with what they think, it happens. Either take it and run with it, get angry and struggle with it, or eventually transfer because it was not the right fit.

If you ever need to address an issue of playing time, a good way to go about that would be to ask just what your role on the team is and if there is anything that you should be focusing on in the meantime. That way, you are not going in there and attacking the coach about how you should be playing and putting them on the defensive. You want it to be an open conversation that allows them to say what they need to say. It also makes you look like you are trying to get better and work things out (which will also likely be the case as well). You may get an inconclusive or cryptic response, which is certainly not helpful. You may have to talk to assistant coaches for more information. If speaking with your coaches does not help, then the program may not be the right fit for you.

Entrance and exit meetings are an important part of your relationship with your coaches. Entrance meetings are where you talk about what you have done in the off season or during your time off. These are typically fairly casual and not too high stress. Coach would usually talk about his expectations for the year and you would be in and out in five minutes. Typically, this would be about the same for both fall and spring entrance meetings.

Exit meetings are an entirely different beast. My experience could be different than other experiences, but it is important to be prepared either way. For our exit meeting Coach would have us do these paper self-assessments. These assessments would go over a variety of things athletically and personally related (doing the right thing, good attitude, etc). I am fairly self-aware, and I would answer pretty close to how Coach would assess me. There could be times where you may be asked about teammates or situations that happened. You can answer those questions at your discretion, but for some reason Coach always seemed to know what was happening with the team.

If you truly believe something or someone is hurting the team, you should bring it up to your coach. Typically, it helps if you have more than one person who can go with you to the coaching staff. However, do not take the power of numbers or bringing something up to the coaches lightly. When you are in college, you are an adult. The first thing you should do is bring up the issue with the individual or the team and then bring it up to the coach as a last resort. Be an adult about things; this is not high school.

Transferring or leaving your sport all together is nothing to be ashamed about. There are tons of reasons that athletes transfer schools or separate themselves from their sport. Sometimes athletes may have been misled or were not in the right place for their own personal situation.

Transferring is easier than ever now because of the online portal. Talk to your coach and compliance office if you are wanting to transfer from your school. There are many rules surrounding transfers and whether you will be immediately eligible to play or not. It is best to get informed from your institution's compliance office who will be able to help you.

If you decide to transfer or stop playing, you have college experience under your belt to make a potentially more informed decision about what you want. You may have different insight or beliefs now than when you were initially looking at colleges in high school. This could range from coaching style, playing time, personalities of teammates, or academics itself. You should be in a situation that is best for you personally, academically, and athletically. At the end of the day, it is about what you want (not anybody else) and what will make you successful in the long run.

CHAPTER SIX
Team Issues

While you are going to meet some of the people who will become your best friends, not everything will be easy all the time. Remember, you will not be friends with everyone on the team. When I was playing, there were times that I had maybe said a handful of sentences to one or two teammates over a full season. We all would respect each other, but there was no reason for us to typically interact. Not everyone's personalities click and that is okay.

Issues can arise because there are so many different personalities on your team no matter how big or small. These can range from little squabbles to big blowouts over a multitude of things ranging from your sport to personal issues. Altercations can happen in the locker room, during practice, or even games. You can either choose to be a part of the drama or ignore it. If you are involved, do your best to keep it outside of team areas. While not every year was drama filled, I certainly did see a fair share of it over my four years. It is great if you can make it out of a season without any drama because it can destroy a team from the inside out.

One year, we just had drama the whole season. It came to a point where we, as a team, had to sit in a circle and let everyone vent out their pent up anger. It was interesting because there were multiple pockets of in-fighting. Some I had no idea about. Each individual case had to work themselves out in front of everyone. It was awkward, but by the end of the whole thing, everyone was hugging everything out and apologizing. While it was a surface level apology for some of the individuals, it was a way for everything to get put on the table with a bunch of mediators. The whole team certainly did not have to get involved in individual issues, but all the tension was affecting the team dynamic which made it everyone's business.

Now, the meeting did feel necessary, in theory, for everyone to get on the same page. However, it did not really fix the individual problems. The one good thing is that many realized that people oftentimes are dealing with stuff that they may not know about. This was the place where we truly found out about everyone's dirty laundry. It was good in one sense, but bad in another. From that moment on, there were less awkward moments between certain individuals. It was awkward before, but at least everyone knew what the issues were and what topics to stay away from.

It is not uncommon to see an individual who is having a hard time dealing with the stress of school, softball, and family or health issues. There are some who willingly will disclose what is happening in their life; there are also some who may not. I had a teammate who was acting weird for a few days and I found out that her mother was diagnosed with cancer. You never know what someone could be going through. It is important to respect your teammates and allow them to tell what is going on if they want; do not just prod them for information.

Being a student-athlete, you are around your teammates nearly every day for at least a couple hours a day, especially on a regular team sport. Sometimes you will get on people's nerves and they will get on your nerves. You will have to learn when it is necessary to separate yourself from a situation or an individual if everything becomes too much. I have seen screaming matches between two who simply got on each other's nerves. It is something that occasionally happens when you are around your teammates 24/7 especially during the season. However, do not let this scare you, there were plenty of teams that we did not want the year to end because it was so fun.

You need to know who your friends are on the team and be careful about what you say to certain people. Refrain from "talking crap" because typically it winds up biting you in the butt especially if you talk to or around the wrong person. Keep the negative energy away, there really is no place for it on any team, not just in college. Your goal is to win a national championship and a negative attitude is not going to help you win. Yes, it sucks if someone else is playing over you that may not necessarily be better than you; sometimes politics is involved. Just do what you do normally, work hard, and show that there should not be any reason for them to keep you out of the lineup. Sometimes, you may be just shit outta luck and you will have to look at your options after the season.

Just remember as a college athlete, you are an adult dealing with adults. You do not have to like every single person on your team, but you should respect them. Even if it is to the point where you do not respect them, figure it out to where it does not affect what you do on the field. Do not let any pent-up anger take hold on the field. It not only is going to affect you and your playing, but possibly other teammates and therefore the rest of the dynamic of the team.

If you ever have any issues, with anybody, that leads to harassment, assault, or any other types of claims where you feel you may be in danger. Do not be afraid to go to the police to file a report. Also move up the chain to your coaching staff, athletic administration, and dean's office. If the issue is extremely serious and ignored, there could be other methods to get the issue resolved.

CHAPTER SEVEN
Travel

Traveling is an exciting part about playing college sports. Especially if you are in a conference where you are able to travel across the country. Sometimes, it can be someone's first time on a plane. I am sure that my experience is similar to other Power 5 conferences, but obviously not every school has the same funding. The funding that some SEC schools have is insane compared to some other conferences.

Regardless of whether you are traveling by bus or by plane to away games, it can take a toll on you if you are not prepared. Traveling was always my favorite part of playing ball because we got to experience so many different climates and see other schools across the country.

You may have long bus rides that are 6 hours plus. Every year, we would take a bus to Palm Springs from Tucson. It was a trip that truly marked the beginning of the season. About halfway through the drive, we would do bus karaoke. This is where people would put headphones in and sing their hearts out. You can tell a lot about people's personalities by the songs that they sing. Every team does different activities to keep themselves occupied on long trips. Some teams have moved from bus karaoke to making dance videos for social media. Whatever keeps you occupied and active on these trips because some can be long.

One year on the Palm Springs bus trip, someone asked for a water bottle and I tried to throw it across the bus. When I released the bottle, I knew it was not going to be good. In slow motion the bottle hit the ceiling and hit one of my teammates who was sleeping in the face. My teammate woke up for two seconds and fell back asleep, but I was so scared because she was not a good person to upset. Luckily, it all wound up okay because she was more mad that she got woken up and was surprised about what had happened.

On bus and plane rides, if you can, try to take the time to catch up on homework or study. Do not get locked into just listening to music, watching a tv show, or sleeping on the bus if you have a lot of homework that you have to catch up on. If you are able to, be productive so you make progress or finish your work before you practice or play. That way you do not have to worry about homework during the rest of your trip.

However, there are many who get car sick or are unable to focus if they try to read in a moving vehicle. Take care of yourself and relax on your way to your destination; when you have off time in the hotel, then do your homework. Ultimately, the way that you decide to study on the road is individual, but what I found successful was using time during plane or long bus rides for homework. Then in my free time, I was searching for a new television show to watch.

Some athletes may have study hall on the road. Typically, it will happen during downtime before games or after games. It just depends on your program and your personal academic plan. If you do not have study hall on the road and you are on your own, do not forget to take a brain break after about forty minutes for about five minutes There is a lot of stress between school, sports, and travel. Your brain needs a short distraction sometimes.

If you think that traveling to play is going to be a vacation, you are mistaken. It truly depends on your coach if you will be allowed outside the hotel or not to go places like the mall or other attractions nearby. Some coaches like for their players to be able to stretch their legs and go on walks. When games were later in the evenings, Coach would almost encourage doing something like this (as opposed to sleeping all day). One year, my roommate, some of our managers, and I walked to a museum across the street from our hotel. Every single time we left the hotel, Coach would always request that we tell him where we were going, with whom, and to text him when we came back. It is important to be honest and always ask before leaving if you have a similar policy. Do not be the person that blows it for the rest of the team when it comes to leaving the hotel.

Occasionally, your coaches may let you see the flair of the city for a few hours. For example, we were able to visit the Pike Place Fish Market for lunch and were given an hour or two to roam around when we went to Washington. In 2019, after we were knocked out of the World Series, we had a series of plane issues and our coaching staff was nice enough to get everyone tickets to the Oklahoma City Zoo while we waited for a new plane. Be grateful to your support staff, always; especially when they take you to sightsee or to other activities. There are a lot of moving parts when it comes to accommodating a whole team/staff on trips like this so be appreciative and patient.

Make sure that you are not late when you are given a deadline to meet up somewhere. Especially on away trips, there are tight timelines for everything. Do not be that person who holds everyone up and if you can, try to be back at the bus or meeting point at least five minutes before the time given. It will make everything easier for everyone involved.

Small things can bring excitement when you are on the road because of how boring it can be if you do not have a ton of homework or things to do. Going to malls can be an exciting excursion. If you can, find little projects you can work on or books you want to read for when you have finished your homework and have downtime. While catching up on television shows is such an easy go-to, do not let it suck up all your time when you could be doing something productive if you choose to. However, we do not live in a perfect world, so catching up on shows usually is the winner.

Before you leave for your trip, it is important to have a well packed suitcase. Make a list of what you want to pack so you do not forget anything, especially if you are a last minute packer. First, pack your uniforms and practice uniforms if you are supposed to pack them. Always double check that you have everything you need for gameday. Once my teammate, forgot her uniform. Luckily, our team had a "manager bag" where there would be extra uniforms and accessories, so everything wound up okay. However, the worst part is telling Coach that you forgot your uniform and that you have a new number for that weekend. Make sure you always have all your uniforms.

After uniforms, the next important things are medications; especially birth control for the ladies and underwear. You can borrow nearly everything else, but those two things. After that, clothing wise, you would want to pack shirts, shorts, pants, socks, sports bras (if needed), and slide shoes. Just stuff you can lounge in and/or sleep in. If you like to dress up for the occasional time you may be able to go out with family or friends, bring jeans and a nice top. Usually, the team as a whole will not be wearing fancy clothing when going out to dinner unless it is requested by the coaching staff.

When it comes to toiletries, bring toothbrush, toothpaste, hairbrush, and hair products. The hair products are especially important if you do not like the hotel equivalent. If you like to do game-day hair and makeup do not forget hairspray, any hair tools, or makeup that you may need to get the job done.

Regardless of what your pre-game routine is, you will want to have everything in one space for you to be able to grab and go week in and week out during the season. I would keep travel toiletries in my suitcase, so it was always there. Everything else, I would have in a bag that would easily be able to transport from our team room at the field to my suitcase at home. When you are traveling nearly every other weekend, you are going to be worried about bigger things than toiletries and underwear. Put the things that you may easily forget in your suitcase beforehand.

Depending on your program, you may get to pick your roommates or have them randomly assigned. Throughout my four years, there was a variance in roommate options. One year, we switched often and another year we got to pick. If you are rooming with one of your friends, it is really fun. However, if you are with someone you are not as close with, you may just be sitting in silence when you two are in the room together.

It is important to understand others' roommate style. Some are messy and others are clean; some like the room cold and others do not. You need to be with someone that is compatible, or it may be necessary to speak with your coach about switching roommates.

One of the perks about being on the road is that schools will typically give per-diem for meals that they did not provide. Sometimes schools will provide all meals and not really give any per-diem. However, on the occasion that they do, it is fantastic. I would often try and save the money for my personal endeavors, just like some of my teammates. Every dollar counts when you do not have a real job. Sometimes we would get a lot of money, at least a lot of money for someone who does not have any, and I would only use half of it on meals and save the other half. It was nice to have a little extra money.

If you truly are trying to save up the per diem, make sure that you eat enough and then save up from there. Even saving ten dollars from each trip will add up after a while. At the end of the day, do not purchase yourself flaming mignon just because you can.

CHAPTER EIGHT
Scholarships

Scholarships are a touchy subject that people often are not honest about. Usually when you talk to people who received an athletic scholarship, they will say that they have a full ride. I know I have told people that, even though it was not technically the case. I am just going to use the example of softball because that is what I know. There are 12 scholarships allotted for an entire team. The lowest roster number I have been a part of was 18 and the highest was 22. As you can see, that number does not match up with the amount of scholarships allotted.

Some kids will sign for full scholarship, others for partial or just books. Some kids get nothing but academic money or grants they are able to find. There is an array of how money can be allotted. The better grades and test scores you get in high school, the better your chances are at getting a higher academic scholarship. It makes you more valuable because then coaches are able to cut scholarships into pieces since you are able to receive academic scholarship money from the school.

Scholarships are typically signed year to year, while academic scholarships usually run the course of eight semesters as long as your grade point average (GPA) is kept up. There are no guarantees that you receive the same amount of athletic money all four years because coaches can change the amount of money you receive based on performance. It does mean that if you do not perform, you could get your scholarship cut. The opposite is true as well. One could go from a walk-on, receiving no monetary support from athletics to a full scholarship the next year. It is important to maintain an open relationship with your coaches about scholarship money if your performance is not what was expected, or it exceeds expectations.

Scholarship money has a few different places where it can be dispersed. Usually, tuition and books are paid through the bursar's office. Room and board can be distributed as a check to the individual or directly to each channel (depending on the school). The check sizes can vary year to year and depend on whether you live in the dorms or not. It is important to budget because finances can get tight when you are paying for living expenses.

I have had teammates who many times came close to not making rent because they would spend their money on non-essential items first. Make sure you are aware of what period of time the checks are supposed to cover. You do not want to be running on pennies when it gets to the end of that cycle. In addition, I have heard of instances when a student-athlete accidentally got overpaid and they went and spent the money right away on something. They were asked by the school to give back the money, and they had to return what they had purchased. You want to be smart with your money. It is okay to occasionally splurge, but do not forget about the important things first.

When creating a budget, the first thing that your money should go to is rent and utilities which are fixed costs. I had multiple checking accounts to help me with my funds. One checking account is where the money for my fixed costs would go. Then I would split the remaining amount between 70/30 between my second checking account and my savings. That second checking account would serve for food and other things that I would want/need to purchase.

Every student-athlete at my university was given the opportunity to eat breakfast 6 days a week during the school year at a school run cafeteria. As I progressed throughout my career, our support staff was great in providing snacks available midday in our training-center. We were also fortunate enough to receive meals after practice. Many other universities offer accommodations similar to this. Being given meals and snacks is helpful to cut down on food costs if you are offered options like this.

If you are not so fortunate to receive meals from your university, there are still ways to budget for meals. It starts with cooking at home or in the dorms rather than eating out. My freshman year, we only received breakfast and I ate out a lot because I was not familiar with the kitchen. As the year progressed, I wanted to cut down on costs, so I began trying to "cook" in the dorm kitchen. After a series of disasters, that turned into eating prepackaged meals and rotisserie chickens from the grocery store. In the following years, I turned to online sources for meal ideas, got a slow cooker, and ate a lot of pasta. All in all, cooking is cheaper than eating fast food, especially if you are able to meal prep for days ahead of time.

Deciding where you are going to live is a big task. Staying in the dorms is a way to meet people and be close to campus. Some schools require freshmen to stay in the dorms, so you may not get much of a choice. There is not a lot of privacy for those who live in the dorms. Oftentimes, there are shared bathrooms between an entire hall. I was lucky and was in a part of the dorm where my roommate and I shared a bathroom between one other room. However, there were times where people would be loud at all times; slamming doors, yelling, and anything else you could think of. Definitely take the time to research all the dorms and amenities to see which one would be your best fit.

Living off campus can also be an option for freshmen at certain universities. The off-campus options can be cheaper depending on what part of the country you are going to school. The off-campus options may also have more amenities than the dorms as well. Some of my teammates lived a little bit farther from campus, but they had a nice place for much cheaper. I gave up having a nice place to live close to campus. Everything is highly personal, and it depends on what you want. There are nice, expensive high rises that tend to be on campuses, but even those have drawbacks with slow elevators, loud parties, and sometimes even backed up plumbing (it happened at UofA one year). You are a college kid; a baller on a budget, just remember, you will not be in your living quarters a lot. All you truly need is a place to sleep, eat, and put your stuff. To each their own, but just remember you are responsible for yourself since you are an adult.

Picking who your roommates are is an exciting part about being away from home, especially if you have a roommate(s) that you vibe with. It is important to have compatible roommates when it comes to your living situation. While you may be inclined to room with your best friend, it may not be the best for your relationship based on how they act at home. If you like a quiet home environment, you probably will not want someone playing loud music at all hours. Other people may have standards of cleanliness that you do not agree with.

Typically, the dishes or trash can drive people up the wall. So it is important to have a conversation with who you are living with in order to hash out the details and if it would be a good fit. If you do not want to room with any of your teammates, usually schools have a roommate matching service. Your coaches may be able to help you find roommates from other sports teams as well.

Many of my teammates would live together with three or four in a house. Sometimes they were good experiences, sometimes they were not. People can get on each other's nerves since not only do they have to be with each other at practice all day, but also at home. Other drama can arise from tasks like doing the dishes or taking out the trash. I loved going to my teammates' houses to have fun with them, but I was not sure that being with them literally 24/7 would be the best for me. It really is a personal choice and every team and individual situation is different. If everyone in the house truly gets along then great, but just be aware that there may be some light squabbles every so often.

I had a unique roommate experience during my time in college. Originally, I was supposed to be a roommate with a non-athlete that I met on a matching service who was from around where I lived. We put our information into the dorm portal and a few weeks later, I found out I was in a different dorm with one of my teammates. This was a surprise because I was not expecting to be with my teammate and my original roommate was not expecting to be with someone random. This happened because there were too many athletes in the original dorm we chose. All our teammates were in the other dorm, but us. The only benefit was that our dorm was the summer dorm that everyone stayed in for post-season and that we shared a bathroom with one other room instead of a whole hall.

The next year, I moved out of the dorms into a house with a girl from the track and field team. It was great, until halfway through the year, she got married and left me. We eventually found a replacement roommate who was in town working for the National Guard. We were lucky that we were able to find someone to fill that spot and everything worked itself out. The next school year, I moved in with a friend from a club I was into a different house nearby.

My senior year was an interesting one, because my sister began her first year of college and we became roommates in the house I was in the year prior. In the beginning of the spring, our house was broken into and we wound up moving to an apartment complex closer to the school that was furnished. That situation was terrifying because my sister and her friends were in the house and left for thirty minutes. Then when they came home, the front door was wide open, and the back gate was forced open. The criminals entered the house through a window in my sister's room that they screwed open. So, we assume that they were definitely watching the house which gives me chills just to think about.

They took valuables like a laptop, jewelry cases, and a camera. I was the saddest about my PAC-12 ring that was in the jewelry case. They even used our pillowcases to hold their loot. We were able to get out of our lease because of the lack of safety measures in place at our house. When looking for a place to live, you need to look at the area and crime rates. Some areas are better than others. There should always be safety measures in place to protect you where you live. Many houses where I was had bars on the windows and a lot of light fixtures. It is better to be overcautious than not cautious at all.

All in all, when it comes to creating a budget, know where your priorities lie. If you want to spend some extra money on a hobby, then cut out an extra fast food meal and instead eat at home. Stick to your budget and if you go over it, make sure what you are purchasing is necessary and adjust for the next month. These skills are important to develop in college to eventually take with you into the real world.

CHAPTER NINE
Injuries

Injuries are an unfortunate part of the game. Injuries do not discriminate on who gets them either. They can happen to the best player on the team or someone who does not see playing time. I was one of the lucky few who did not have many injuries during my entire playing career. My junior year of high school, I had an ankle injury from pitching overuse, and I had to get a cortisone shot. The summer before my freshman year of college, I sprained my ankle during a game when I stepped in a hole while trying to back up the catcher. Instead of spending the rest of the night watching fireworks, I spent my fourth of July at an urgent care. Luckily, I was able to recover before the fall season of my freshman year.

In college, the most severe injury that I had was my senior year when I got hit in the face with the ball when I was batting. I was not wearing a facemask, but the way that the ball deflected off the top of my helmet into my eye was just enough that the only damage it caused was a black eye. It was a miracle that I came out with no concussion and nothing broken or fractured. My parents watched that happen on television. They were obviously extremely worried because they were not able to contact me until after the game.

Injuries

I want to say that I ultimately assumed the risks when I stepped in the box without a faceguard. When it comes to protective gear, if you have the choice, you should be able to make an informed decision on what you decide to use. Listen to your trainers and coaching staff and see what they suggest.

Some injuries are season ending. Some injuries are nagging, and you have to play through them. For instance, shin splints are horrible, but they are something that many athletes play through. It is important that you are taking care of yourself and taking the proper precautions for your body. If that means you are in the training room twice a day getting worked on or doing therapeutic exercises, then so be it. You want to be able to prep your body and keep it safe for the tasks that you have to accomplish day in and day out.

Regardless of the type of injury, you should listen to and have open communication with your trainer and coaches about your health plan. It is also important to know when you need to stop. There may be a time where you have to override a trainer or coach because your body may be in too much pain beyond pushing through. It may not be worth putting your body through that much stress/pain for the longevity of your sports career and for functionality in life after sports.

When it comes to big injuries, the training plan can get discouraging especially if you have to sit out for a couple of months to a year. Use the resources you have, such as psychologists and training staff. Trust the process and try not to rush into anything. Listen to your trainers because they ultimately want to protect you and the longevity of your playing career. Do not be afraid during your time off the field/court/pool to find other things that you are interested in to get your mind off of rehabbing.

Injuries are the worst part of being an athlete. No one wants to be away from their team or sport. If/when they happen make sure that you are taking care of yourself and have support that you are able to talk to if you need it. Communicate with your coaches because while the trainer clears you to play, your coach has the ultimate decision about putting you in the lineup. The first thing that is important is you and your well-being, second being your academics and sport. Do not forget that.

CHAPTER TEN
Social Life

Good luck.

Just kidding. College is a place where you will have interesting experiences with many different people. Your interactions with people will likely begin with the other athletes, but also expand to those you meet in classes or clubs. You should not feel that you are only exclusive to the athletes and that non-athlete regular people (NARPs) are not cool. At the end of the day, you should be able to explore and meet people from all different walks of life. Having a diverse group of acquaintances or friends can help you out after your college and athletic days are behind you.

College is a great place to explore your interests because campuses offer an abundance of clubs to fit any niche. There are often multiple clubs that cover similar subjects, so just because you may not like one club does not mean you will not like another. I was in a multitude of clubs and it allowed me to meet people outside of the sports bubble.

Club rush was an exciting time for me every year because I was able to see all the different organizations I could join in one place. While there were many I was interested in, I was not always able to make meetings because of practice or other club meetings. One club that I was consistently in all four years was student radio. I had a show nearly every week in the mornings after workouts during the school year for four years. The people and experiences were great to build contacts and grow in my public speaking skills.

I was in a political club consistently for my first two years of college and then members graduated, and I did not connect with the new people as much anymore. I stopped attending meetings, but I was still around and would go to the occasional event. Other organizations I was in included an ambassador program and an honorary. The ambassador program was a part of the alumni association and the other was a sports honorary intended for NARPs who loved our college sports team. These groups both required an application and interview.

The ambassador program was awesome for life skills development and interaction with donors. The honorary was a different story. While I did not click with everyone in that club, I did make a few good friends and it had some fun moments. I also dabbled in the ballroom club for a semester and participated in a ballroom competition.

If you are unable to find a club hosted by your school, I encourage you to look at community groups. Since my freshman year of college, I have been dancing a type of swing called west coast swing. This became a two time a week obsession during the off season. Eventually, I became a board member of Tucson Swing Dance Club.

To match my love for local government/politics, my senior year, I was appointed as an advisory commissioner to the Tucson Human Rights Commission. All these activities were a great experience to meet people of various demographics and age groups. I was glad to be able to find and connect with people that were able to help me grow.

While it sounds like I was doing a lot, which I was, it was important for me to learn when it was too much. There were times where I knew it was a bad idea to go to a dance or stay out late after a meeting. When softball season was in full swing, I had to cut back on a lot of my activities. It is important to be able to know your limits. Playing college sports is already hard enough, but then you add maintaining a good GPA, and trying to have a social life. Eventually, something is going to have to give in order to be a functioning individual. I would always tell people that if you like something enough, you will find time for it. While some activities may have obvious time conflicts, there are sometimes alternatives available for you. Over time, you will learn your limit to be able to balance everything effectively.

College is the best time to be able to try activities you have never tried before. You are not being policed by your parents or anyone during your free time. In your free time you are truly free to do whatever you like. If this means joining a painting club, then so be it. I am such a huge proponent of using thc four/five years of undergraduate to go outside of your box because you will never be in a space like this again. You are able to dabble in many things and if you simply do not like what you have tried, you do not have to do it again. Simple as that.

While playing sports is an important part of your college, finding something that you like outside of your sport is important because you will not be an athlete forever. Eventually, your career is going to end, and you may need another outlet to express yourself.

Going out and partying is also a part of college. This is what parents do not want to hear about, but too bad, partying happens in college. It is a part of the culture and I thought it would be doing an injustice to ignore the fact that it happens. I want to first mention that if you are under 21 and live in America, consumption and possession of alcohol is illegal. If you are caught, you can face legal ramifications such as fines or a driver's license suspension. Your actions have consequences. Teams have rules. If you break those rules and your coaches find out, which they probably will, you could be suspended or removed from the team. There is no free pass just because you might be a superstar. Some things, like use and abuse of alcohol and especially drugs, are just not worth the end of your career.

Now that I have scared you, moving onto the good stuff.

Typical social events can range from house parties on Saturday nights to tailgates before football games. These events are a really good place to meet people and have some fun. While alcohol is usually involved, I was more concerned with being with my teammates and meeting people rather than the drinking.

Do not feel like you have to do anything just because people try to coax you on. Honestly, at least what I have seen, people are pretty respectful or will just go back to doing their own thing if you are adamant about not drinking. If you do engage in drinking, be smart about it. If someone tells you to stop drinking, it is probably for your own good. It is important to know your limits to prevent yourself from acting like an idiot. Not every town's authority is lenient for underage drinking and wild parties, especially when they might recognize who you are. You may catch police on a good day or a bad day, but it is best to not find out.

The best advice that I can give about the party culture is to be smart and not drink or take anything when you do not know where it is from or what it is.

Athletes do host their own parties and they are often fun because you get to meet all the other athletes! It can be a really cool experience, especially if your university has high profile athletes. Things can get weird if drama happens and then you have to see all those same people in the athlete common areas. That comes with the turf, though.

I have seen these athlete parties get out of hand. One summer, my teammate threw the party of the summer at her house. This party was originally intended for the athletes who were in summer school. The party grew in size tremendously with people no one knew just showing up. We had door guards, but eventually that stopped working. After a couple of hours, the police were called because of an obvious noise complaint. It was definitely annoying and a risk having a bunch of people in the house that we did not know, but the party was epic. The clean up sucked though.

In the aftermath of this event my teammate had to take responsibility for what she had done. She was in really good standing with the athletic department and she called administration to tell them what had happened. There was no one who had a minor in possession or driving under the influence and the only thing that happened was a "red tag" (a noise complaint). She wound up going to court to fight the fine and the police did not show up, so she won her case.

Parties may be fun, but they can turn serious really fast. The day after the party of the summer, the basketball team threw a party. Someone shot off a gun, but luckily there were no reported injuries. Not everything is sunshine and rainbows, and you have to be careful. At countless other parties, the police showed up and there were a ton of drunk athletes trying to disassociate themselves from the party. As an athlete you do not want to end up on "Page 6" or the front page of the paper for any illicit activity. It really is a bad look and can end in suspension or termination.

To be clear I am not condoning underage drinking, but I am just telling you the reality of the situation. When you turn 21 years old, the bars seem to be safer than house parties. You will likely be over house parties by that time in your life.

Another part of the "do not be stupid rule" applies to social media. Many times, coaches and universities do track student-athletes' social media. If you feel like your parents would not be proud or want to read what you are posting online, you probably do not want your coaches to read it either. Even when it is private, you cannot be sure that it does not get out. You just never know, just be smart. One of our athletic directors, every year at the back to school barbeque, would show social media comments that were inappropriate from student-athletes in the year prior. It was really funny, I mean really funny, but you did not want to end up on the jumbotron for everyone and your coaches to see.

Being a student-athlete puts you on a pedestal and it is possible that you may get messages from random people. You do not have to feel obligated to respond to these messages, especially if they are inappropriate. I have gotten my fair share of weird messages. One guy found me on social media after he saw me at a restaurant because I was wearing my practice shorts that said "Arizona Softball" on them. In his message he wrote that he thought that I was cute, and he wanted to take me out. Half of it was spelled wrong with incorrect grammar which was hilarious, and my teammates thought it was comical. Needless to say, I did not respond.

Many of our games during the season were on television and therefore it puts us out more in the public eye. If you are in a high-profile sport at your university, just know that you may receive comments or messages that may not be favorable all the time if you have a public profile. If you desire to keep your social media private, then only accept people that you really know. If the messages you get ever escalate to where you feel threatened, block the individual and let your coaches and/or a trusted adult know. They should be able to help you if legal action needs to be taken. Social media is how people tend to communicate nowadays. Not only is it how you are able to show the world what you are doing, it is also how you are able to see what others are doing and connect with them. Social media can be used positively to help set yourself up post-college to establish your personal brand. However, it can also be used in a negative way to hurt you and your reputation. You represent not only yourself and your family, but also your university.

CHAPTER ELEVEN
Faith

If you are religious or semi-religious, I think it is important to stay connected with that community while you are a student-athlete. College is a great place to grow and meet people in your religion or others if you are exploring. There are many different resources at many colleges for student-athletes and NARPs ranging from various on-campus groups to hangouts off campus. These places can offer a home away from home by giving mental and physical support to students as well as food.

I am Jewish and being connected to the Jewish community is important for me. I wanted to go to a University that had a Jewish presence because it was important to know that I would always have a place to go to for the holidays. I would often spend my Friday nights at Shabbat dinners and attend synagogue during the holidays. Having a community like this was able to help create extra stability in my life. It was nice to be able to be around like-minded people and have a hearty debate over dinner. Through these organizations, I was also able to learn more about my religion and the life lessons that come from that through the programming that they offered. While the days as a student-athlete are busy, members of religious organizations will gladly make time to meet with you whenever you are free.

Some of my teammates would often host religious meetings at their house. There were also athletes who would meet during breakfast or in between breaks to talk about religion. People are willing to have conversations and oftentimes there are those who are paid to facilitate and teach.

Being Jewish, there are certain holidays or customs that not everyone would understand. However, people are normally respectful when asking about such things and are genuinely curious most of the time. One holiday that is especially important to me is Yom Kippur. Typically, it would somehow fall on a day where we would have only weights and I would makeup that session on a different day.

One year, we had a practice on Yom Kippur and I asked for it off with another Jewish teammate. Coach said, "Of course." He wound up moving that practice to a Saturday so everyone could be there. We did not think he would change the whole practice because two of us would not be attending. Little did I know that a few of my teammates were going to go home that weekend and we, unfortunately, ruined their travel plans. Whoops, but there was nothing anyone could do about it.

If your faith is important to you or you want to inquire more about it during your time in college, there are plenty of resources available for you. First, ask your teammates (and sometimes even coaches) if they know of any meetings or events and if not, then look at your school's club directory. If you are able to get involved that way then great and if there is a religious organization tailored to athletes, then even better.

CHAPTER TWELVE

Life Skills

If your school offers life skills programming, especially through the athletic department, you need to take advantage of it. Do not just brush off emails and reminders. You may not have the time during your college career to be able to have multitudes of these experiences in real life. These programs teach you skills in a controlled manner that will benefit you in the long run.

Some of my teammates were sad that they did not try to attend these programs earlier in their college career. The earlier that you are able to begin career development, the better. That way you have time to learn and grow rather than attempting to cram all the information in when you are trying to get internships or jobs later on.

I was the queen of attending these life skills programs throughout my whole career. These classes could range from budgeting to resume and cover letter classes. Typically, food would be provided to help bribe student-athletes to attend. After a while, I got sick of eating pizza every time and I would go for the content rather than the pizza. The programming allowed me to become educated in a plethora of topics that are important once college is over.

Along with life skills, many schools also have leadership programs you are able to be a part of. My school had Peer Athletic Leaders (PAL) and Student Athlete Advisory Committee (SAAC). PAL was a great jumpstart for any athlete to help develop their leadership skills and meet other athletes. Anyone was able to join PAL regardless of year in school or leadership level. Guest speakers would always join us and we would often do team-building ice-breakers. If one truly wanted to be recognized as a member of PAL they would have to attend a certain number of meetings or they would have had to do a special project. If your school has something similar, I would recommend at least attending meetings.

All schools will have SAAC or a version of it, but every school runs it differently. My school had only one representative from every sport who would attend SAAC meetings twice a month; one official and one unofficial. Either the coach would select a representative or someone from the team would apply. SAAC is similar to student government. Your team's representative reports on things that are going on with your team at the SAAC meetings. Student-athletes are able to air grievances they have with their coaches or school. We would also vote on rule changes from the school, conference, or overall governing body. If you are able to be a member of SAAC, it can be an exciting experience. Some SAACs host events for their student athletes. It just depends on the school, but it is what you make it.

My junior year was my first year on SAAC. I was able to go to San Francisco, all expenses paid, to go to the PAC-12 SAAC Conference. It was such an amazing experience because I was able to get to know people from outside my sport and school. I learned all about what other schools do to get students engaged and projects that their respective SAACs work on. We also did a community service project, where we helped host a ping pong tournament at a community center in the Tenderloin district. It was an extremely humbling experience. If you have the ability to go on a trip similar to this, do not hesitate to apply. It is something you will not regret.

Community service not only is good for character building, but you also give back to the community that gives you so much. Your team may do community service together or you may have opportunities to go out and do it on your own. If you are given the opportunity to help out and you are free, you should do it. Nothing feels better than helping out the community that supports you and your teammates. I participated in many different types of community service opportunities that ranged from speaking at schools to visiting troops on the Air Force base to pulling buffelgrass. There are plenty of options and oftentimes, the school is able to set you up with opportunities.

All of these programs that are often offered by schools are able to help you gain experience to build your resume. What athletes typically lack in job experience, could be made up in leadership roles and proper explanation of the dedication and skills you learned from being a student athlete.

It is crucial to find an internship during your college experience. Do not let your four years go by and then realize that you have to enter the work force with no work experience. An internship or fellowship is by far one of the most crucial things you can do in college to help get a job post-college. If you are able to find a summer internship, great, but if you are not able to because of your schedule, there are also fall and spring internships. There are even places that will work with your school/practice schedule.

Obtaining an internship post-college is typically hard to come by without still being enrolled in school.

The fall of my sophomore year, I interned at the Tucson Hispanic Chamber of Commerce. I did some social media work and took minutes at their meetings. I would go into their office once or twice a week and I learned a lot about how they help out local businesses and the importance of their work. This was a great starter internship for me, especially because they were able to work with my schedule. I also had a great supervisor who was really able to walk me through various graphic design platforms that I still utilize today. There are always local organizations that are looking for help and sometimes all it takes is an email.

The internship at the Tucson Hispanic Chamber of Commerce was able to lay the groundwork for my internship at Nike's World Headquarters. In the summer of 2018, I had an amazing opportunity to go to Beaverton, Oregon and work in Nike's brand marketing department. There, I was able to connect with a former Arizona softball player and an alumni network. Even though I had to earn my spot for the internship, I credit the opportunity to the athletic department and their relationship as a Nike school.

Being thrust into the real-world experience at Nike was where I truly learned a lot about myself and where I could be beneficial to a company. While Nike was not necessarily in the space where I ultimately wanted to be, I learned so much during my time and I am forever appreciative that I was able to experience it. Nike was actually the first place where I have failed, aside from sports. By failed, I mean told to go back to the drawing board on multiple occasions. There were often many moving parts and I am humbled that I was able to be around brilliant minds and learn how they process information.

My internship allowed me to expand my capabilities, but not every internship is bound to be groundbreaking. You will, though, learn about what you like in a work environment and what you do not like. Internships are important to figure out what you want to do. You may even find out that you may not actually want to do what you thought. There is a lot of trial and error. Being in college is great because you have the time to figure it out. It especially helps if you do it early on in your academic career.

Internships can be like gold to some individuals. At some companies, if you perform well during an internship there could be a chance it leads to a job in the future. Take every opportunity you get seriously and put out your best work, even if the task at hand seems dumb. Do not ever write people off, especially individuals who are trying to help you. You never know where you may see someone again.

CHAPTER THIRTEEN
Academics

Whether you like it or not, you will have to go to class. Your governing body and your college will have GPA requirements. Essentially, if you do not have a high enough GPA, you will not play. With all of the resources that the schools will give you, at least in the PAC12/SEC and other Power 5 conferences that I have seen, you will have to deliberately try to not study and waste time in study hall to not get the minimum GPA. Usually the culprit for not getting decent enough grades is simply not attending classes or studying material.

You are a student first regardless of what sport you play. That is why the term is student-athlete not athlete-student. Most student-athletes do not go on to play professional sports and use college to help pay for school. Even those who do go on to play professionally have a timeline on their careers; eventually they will have to find something else to do. It is helpful if they have a degree to fall back on or usable and a substantial amount of credits to attain a degree at a later date.

If your school provides it, you may be able to receive tutoring help through your athletic department. They may offer group or individual tutoring. You should always take the tutoring if it is offered because your tutor would be able to help with most questions you may have. If there are not any tutors available for class, you may have to specially request one or find study groups or tutors through your individual college.

Quite honestly, college classes are like fancy high school classes. You still go to a classroom and listen to a professor speak for typically an hour. There are more hands-on courses that can take place in labs. May schools offer hybrid classes that are half online and half in person. Homework or papers are assigned depending on the professors. Some professors have pop quizzes or unit quizzes, but a majority have at the very least a midterm and final. You will also have to learn to hone in your writing because papers can also often hold a significant amount of weight on a grade.

The best thing about college courses is that you receive a syllabus for the entire semester. It essentially lays out not only the expectations for the class, but it also has the schedule for readings, homework, and exams. Typically, there should be no surprises and you will be able to review everything for the semester and how it lines up with your schedule. If you ever have any questions, review the syllabus first before contacting your professor. Usually, most questions are answered, but if they are not, your professor will be happy to answer you.

For your in-person classes, you will be given a Dean's Excuse to excuse you from classes you will miss during season. It is important to give these to your professors as soon as you receive them, which will be generally about a week before the missed class. At the beginning of the semester we would give our professors a letter with dates of our games. At the end of the first day of class, I would go to each professor and introduce myself. I would inform them I was on the softball team and that I may have to miss class or test due to away games. In my case, the professors were accommodating, and I was able to turn in work early or reschedule a test. There were plenty of times where my teammates had to take a proctored test on the road at the university we were at. It is important to maintain open lines of communication with your professors and athletic-academic counselor if this is your situation.

Some professors may not be as accommodating as others. If there ever is a time when you are told by a professor you will be docked with attendance points or they will not let you make anything up, tell your athletic academic advisor and/or coach immediately. There are faculty athletic representatives whose job is to help in situations like this. These individuals are faculty members who are able to speak to professors on your behalf to help work issues like that out. Do not be afraid to ask for help. Sometimes, if a professor will not accommodate, you may have to take another course. Those situations are few and far between, but they can happen.

To ensure that students are going to class, somc colleges will have class checkers. These class checkers could simply be your counselor, but they can also be plain clothed individuals in the class that you may not necessarily know. Typically, if someone is known to skip class, a class checker will be deployed on a regular basis. However, even if you do not skip class, a class checker can come by at any time and you will get in trouble if you are not there and you are not excused.

When I was in college, I had a teammate that was going through some personal issues and stopped going to class. Eventually, her absence was discovered. Some professors vary on whether they take attendance or not every class, but it should not matter. The punishment for my teammate was that she had to go to study hall instead of practice. It was absolutely devastating for her, but athletics has rules on missing class.

Loss of practice time is a minimal punishment, but there can be even larger repercussions such as not being able to play in games. Regardless of the reason, it is best to speak with your academic counselor, trainer, coach, or someone in the athletic department that you trust to talk about what you would need to help your situation if that were to happen.

Never be afraid to ask for help. Your school's support staff wants to help you succeed. They want you to be eligible grades wise so you can play. They want you to be making good choices in your personal life. You will be under a microscope, but it is because you not only represent yourself, but your school. Literally, everywhere you go.

The development of online classes has made learning much more accessible from anywhere which is great for when you are on the road. You do not have to deal with missing classes, but you still have timelines. Make sure you always check the time that assignments or tests are due. Not every teacher puts the time as 11:59PM. Remember, usually the due dates are in local time, so depending on where you are you may have to turn it in "early" to be on time.

The tough thing about online classes is that you are responsible for knowing when assignments are due; there are not always reminders. You must be on top of due dates because they can pile up. If you have multiple online classes, be diligent when you go through the information. I would split my online classes into Monday, Wednesday, Friday or Tuesday, Thursday for a schedule to mimic regular in person classes. Have an academic planner where you take the time to write the due dates for all of your classes. It will help you out in the long run not to mix anything up. My trick was to use the time between in person classes and practice/workouts to do homework or study.

There are some online courses that you may be able to take that are seven weeks long. These classes are typically intense because it fits an entire semester's worth of information in half the time. One time, I had a seven-week course where the professor wanted us to read so many papers that it was nearly impossible in such a short period of time with other classes. Sometimes, it really does feel like a professor thinks their class is the only class you are taking. After a few weeks, you will figure out how to make the class manageable and which readings are the most important to go over. If you are able to work ahead in these classes, use that to your advantage.

My freshman year, I wasted too much time farting around and the weight of my assignments overcame me. I had a panic attack in the study room in my dorm because it felt like I had to accomplish too much in too little time. Following that episode, I had to change how I went about studying various topics, so I made a checklist of everything that I had to accomplish. It made me feel a lot better working down a list because I was able to physically see everything getting done.

To help prevent overload, if you are able to take summer and winter classes, use them to your advantage. Some academic scholarships require 30 credits to be taken during the school year. Taking a summer or winter course can be helpful because you are able to take one less class during your season. There were a few semesters where I was able to take twelve credits instead of fifteen during the season; one time I even took ballet as an elective. It was nice to not have an overload of schoolwork when the season is in full swing.

One summer, I had to takc accounting because it was a prerequisite to one of my minors. The classes were longer than normal and stuffed with information. I would go to the teacher's office hours a few times a week. Being at school during the summer was fun because all I had to focus on was school, working out, and a little bit of occasional hitting practice. Everything is extremely relaxed, and I was able to make some friends in the class and hang out with them outside of school. Along with after school assistance from the teacher, I was also able to receive tutoring from the athletic department.

It is important to know your professors' office hours. Office hours are where you can go into the professor's office and ask questions, receive help or feedback, or just talk to them. These are important not only for relationship building, but if you need help in a class. I have gone into office hours to ask a professor about a paper I wrote and where it could have gone better. I have also gone to office hours for an online teacher to introduce myself and learn a little more about the class. The professor was excited to see someone and was able to give me insight into how to be successful in the course.

A professor may only offer office hours during your practice. If that is the case, send them an email or speak to them in person if you could meet another time. Professors usually can be fairly flexible and want to be able to meet with you and help you out. If an in-person meeting cannot be accommodated, some professors may offer a video chat option, or you may be able to suggest that. The COVID-19 virus has certainly made more professors aware of capabilities that can be done over the internet.

It is important to be aware of the major that you choose in relationship to your sport's schedule. Some programs may make you choose a different academic program because it does not fit into the sport schedule. Do research on your school beforehand with academic counselors about class times. When I was on my unofficial visit, I had meetings with a few academic counselors for various majors I was interested in. I was in love with a pre-law major, but I found out a majority of the classes at the time were in the afternoon during practice, so I opted for Political Science which had a greater variance of class times.

One of my best friends was a journalism major. There were one or two classes that she had during practice. She managed for the most part to work around it by taking some of the time conflicting classes in the summer, but there were times where she would throw a bullpen, leave for class, and come back to practice. Your coaches and athletic academic counselor will likely steer you away from majors with conflicting class times.

If there is something that you want to work around, it is important to let your Coach know and be prepared to have a discussion about it. Remember, at the end of the day, you are more likely going to come out with an academic degree rather than a professional sports contract. There may be other alternative majors that you are able to take that are similar to your original desired major. This often happens in specific health or science majors, which can be replaced with a more general health or science major. This can also be a deciding factor on the school that you attend i.e. heavy academic load where school matters more than the sport.

The selection of a specific major can be a deal-breaker for some about whether they want to play sports in college or just go to school.

Your coaches will be involved with your academics whether you like it or not. They want to make sure that you are eligible and have no issues. Every week Coach would have a meeting with our athletic-academic counselor about our progress in classes. He would come up to us and ask about our classes because he was curious about how everyone felt they were doing in class. Every time he did this, we would get all surprised about how he knew about the paper someone did not turn in or the exam someone got an "A" on. It was a funny sight, but he wanted us to make sure that he was on top of our academics just as much as we should be.

You will be in contact with your athletic-academic counselor quite often. They somehow manage to fit your academic and athletic career together like a puzzle piece. Sometimes, you may butt heads with your academic counselor, but just remember that they are looking out for your best interest. They do what they can to help you stay eligible and help you make the best decisions for your academics and future.

Some athletic programs also have learning-specialists that are like a mentor, tutor, and counselor all rolled into one. I was not in need of a learning specialist, but I still did go to one when I was not able to have a tutor in my subject. I learned so much from the learning specialist because she had a vast education and experience in the topics I was covering in my classes. Over the years, I learned so much from her and it is amazing to have her as a mentor and as someone who I can still reach out to.

One time, there was an occasion where I was accused of plagiarism. Plagiarism is an extremely serious allegation with severe consequences. I could not even fathom that I would get accused of such a thing when I had no intention of committing plagiarism and my work was my own. Needless to say, I was terrified. The second I got the email, my heart dropped, and I emailed my professor back to schedule a meeting after speaking right away to my academic-athletic counselor.

The next morning, I went to Coach's office freaking out because I have never been accused of something so serious. He heard me out and gave me some fatherly advice on how to handle the matter. It was helpful to know that someone was on my side and that he would be there for me if anything else escalated. It is also important to note that it was best that he heard the news from me first. When it comes to speaking to your coach, always get in front of the issue. It is desirable that they are able to hear your side of the story before hearing about it from a third party.

When I had the meeting with the professor, it was the first time I ever met her. She was nice, but got right down to business and explained what happened when the paper went through the scanner. Someone used the exact same sources and quotes as me; it was the craziest thing I had ever seen. I had to explain my argument in my paper to her. To be honest, the essay prompt was rather complex, and I did not understand it too well, so I tried my best to cxplain what I put together in the essay and how it related to the prompt.

The professor told me that the other individual did not email her back and I would receive the benefit of the doubt. That was a huge relief. I never received a follow up email from the professor, so I am assuming that issue was resolved, and I was clear of a plagiarism claim. It is important that if you are ever accused of cheating or plagiarism that you are to follow the proper protocol in response. Honesty is important. Do not make the professor or dean of your college dig for information because the consequences could be as serious as expulsion.

Learning how to do your homework in a proper manner will be one of the best time saving tactics you will takc. I am the opposite of a procrastinator: a precrastinator. I have to do most things well before the due date. Typically, I would start homework the day it was assigned. It is much easier to be a precrastinator if you are working by yourself on a paper or homework. It does not work too well with group projects of more than two people. I would often get frustrated because others would procrastinate, and I thought we would not be able to turn in quality work. Over the years, I have learned some people work on different timelines and it was important to set self-regulated flexible deadlines on group projects. The only thing that you are able to control is what you do.

Being a precrastinator has allowed me to be able to have time for many things without worry. If I had a big essay due in four weeks, a schedule with deadlines for my writing process would be written in my calendar. Week one would be where I would gather multitudes of sources in a document with the link and information from sources copied in. Week two is where I would take those sources and make an outline for the paper. Week three is when the paper would begin to be written on a separate document than the outline and sources. This is so you are able to do a split screen and see what you are working with. The paper will basically write itself at this point since you already have what you want to say and a source to back it up. Week 4 is where you would edit the paper and turn it in. By having the process of writing your paper spread out, it allows you time to be able to work on other assignments, but still be in control of your paper and the deadlines.

If you are a procrastinator, just know that it will make life a little bit harder (unless you like living on the edge). Sometimes you never know when practice could end and by the time you get home, you may have less time than you thought to do all your work. It may feel easy to just push something off until tomorrow, but do not fall into that trap. Time is of the essence. Get your homework done so you are able to just relax and play your sport without having to worry about anything else.

CHAPTER FOURTEEN
Post-College

By the end of my playing career, I definitely accepted the fact and was glad that I was not going to play another year of college softball. I certainly had my fill, but I luckily was able to continue my softball career as a member of the Israeli National Softball Team.

The transition from college student-athlete to regular person was an interesting one and that process often gets left out of conversation.

You will lose or gain weight. For me, I lost all of my muscle mass. When I was in college, I gained about 5-10lbs. These numbers can vary for so many people depending on your sport and the types of workouts. They may try to bulk you up. You could gain weight, but you could also lose weight. After my internship and being active all the time in Oregon, I dropped to 132lbs (which was essentially my average high school weight) and I have stayed there ever since. When I went to play in Europe with the Israeli National Team, that is where I began to notice a difference in my body type because we were not lifting. A month later, I was shocked at what I saw in the mirror. I was so small and lost a majority of my muscle mass; so much that even people

I saw often noticed. It did not look bad either, it was just different.

Your body will change over the course of four years and then change again after you are done playing if you do not keep a similar workout. My teammates and I would always joke that after college we were never going to workout again. Some of us tried that, but then were drawn right back into it because we missed what the feeling was after you finished working out. I began trying activities like yoga, but it is hard for me to stay motivated. I have turned to shorter, high intensity workouts that keep my attention. Luckily, I have dance that keeps me relatively active, but it does not replace high intensity running or lifting.

It can be difficult to find time to exercise when you are adjusting to your new life. You may be working long hours or running from one thing to another. It may only take 10-15 minutes for a bodyweight workout when you wake up during a break, or before bed to get your workout fix in. Hold yourself accountable if you are committing to trying to work out.

I also learned that I cannot eat the same way as I did in college. My body just does not process the food as quickly anymore. Since I am not working out as much, I start to see a little pooch and I freak out. Fortunately, I am able to bounce back, but everyone's body is different. You will have to figure out what is best for you based on your body to live a healthy life. Do not be discouraged if what you are looking at in the mirror right now is not what you want. Rome was not built in a day and having the lifestyle you want is a journey. As much as it pains me to say this, nothing will happen instantly. It takes time and dedication, something that I continue to work on every day.

If you are struggling, check in with your fellow ex-teammates or athletes that you know. You are certainly not ıe only one going through a change in your life. They will kely be able to share their experiences with you. You all ıay be able to work to hold each other accountable.

There is a saying that you do not typically miss things ıtil they are gone. By the time my four years were up, I was ıentally tired of the grind. I was extremely thankful that I ıd the opportunity and proud of how my career turned out, ıt I was glad that I did not have the toll mentally and ıysically anymore. It took about a year for the feeling of ıissing the sport to come back. There is nothing better than ·playing some of your best moments in your head. ometimes, I still have stress dreams about when I got hit in ıe face with the ball or being called to hit in crucial tuations. Your sport will always be a part of you.

The thing that I miss the most about playing college hletics is the people. There is nothing better than a group of ·ople preparing and fighting for the same goal. You will nd out who your real friends are by who you still talk to ter college. I talk to a few of my old teammates, but I do iss the camaraderie of everyone as a team year in and year ıt. While I do not miss the dying in practice and workouts very day, I just missed the shared experiences. Maybe the ıys who produced the "military-like" program really did ıow what they were talking about.

After college, the world really is your oyster. You are nally free of time constraints, except of those of school or ork. I was finally able to do things that I have always anted to do, but was never able to. I participated in a beauty ıgeant/scholarship competition and won the title of Miss ucson. It was something that was definitely out of my ement. Especially with trying to learn to walk properly in ·els. I was able to practice plenty of mock interviews for the terview portion and I even got a dance choreographed for e talent portion.

It truly was an out of this world experience, but if you have something that you are passionate about you should be able to do it. Take a vacation, go to the event or conference you have always wanted to go to. You deserve it and a pat on the back for making it all four years (or five) as a student-athlete.

Finding a job is typically the next thing on the list after finishing school (or more school is after school). If you were able to secure one after an internship, great. Employers are typically looking to hire recent graduates for jobs or post-grad internships in the spring. Apply to as many as you want to. The more that you can get your resume and cover letter out there the better. Make sure that you are tailoring your cover letter and resume to the jobs that you are applying to. I have three versions of my resume to fit various job markets and I personalize my cover letters every single time. It is the little things that matter. Do not be afraid to reach out to people you have networked with about places that may be hiring or for any advice.

I was able to secure a job at a local radio station in the spring of my senior year. It was an excellent place where I was able to learn so much about the industry. However, I did have to get a second job to survive and I became certified to substitute teach in Arizona. This allowed me a lot of flexibility to work when I wanted to and around the radio schedule. I would also give softball lessons to help out the softball players of tomorrow.

Even though I was doing many different things, this is the path of skill sets that I wanted for my future. It is okay if you have to grind a little bit after college for money. If you find a full-time job with benefits, that is fantastic. Not everyone's story and journey are the same.

The label of student-athlete is some people's end all be all. After your playing career is over, that identity will still be there for the rest of your life, but it will likely not be as important as it once was. You have learned great skills from being a student-athlete, like teamwork, communication, and time management to name a few. Take these skills and develop them over the course of college to come out the best you can be.

ACKNOWLEDGEMENTS

The idea of this book came when I was having a conversation with one of my mentors and fellow Arizona alumni, Manny Espinoza. While I did not want to write a complete tell-all of my college career, I decided to do a tell-some to help future student-athletes in their journey.

Thanks to Kathryn Lance, who is an extremely accomplished writer in her own right, for editing and not being afraid to point out the need for clarification.

Thanks to Coach Candrea for believing in me while I was a student-athlete and being kind enough to write the forward of this book. His words have truly inspired generations and I am glad to have been able to be under his wing for four years at Arizona.

Thanks to those who I kept bugging to read my manuscript; especially when I was closer to publishing the book. Your feedback means the world to me. Especially when I

Thanks to all who believed that this book could happen. I really hope that this base level of information was able to give broader knowledge to you or your student athlete

You listen to learn, if you're not listening, you're not learning. If you're not learning, you're not listening. My dad made me recite that every day before I went to school as a kid.

We all should work to do that more.

Made in the USA
Monee, IL
12 November 2020

47387791R00059